UNSURPASSED RELATIONSHIPS IN
WEALTH MANAGEMENT

BANK INSTRUMENTS INVESTMENT PROGRAMS (BIIPS) AND PRIVATE PLACEMENT PROGRAM (PPP)

INDUSTRY OVERVIEW

As Covered Under International Chamber of
Commerce (ICC) Uniform Customs and
Practice for Documentary Credits (UCP 600)

ABOUT THE AUTHOR

I HAVE SOMETHING TO TELL

Sir Patrick was born in Georgetown, Guyana, South America, and resides in the UK. He is a UN Ambassador, Investment banker, philanthropist, and author. Sir Patrick is a renowned leading specialist in the debt capital markets, private placements, derivatives, and futures trading. As a distinguished trader on Wall Street, he has worked with multiple top banks such as Wells Fargo, Deutsche Bank, Credit Agricole CIB, Merrill Lynch, and others. He has established and managed Hedge Funds such as The Tiger Fund and became a notable Fund Manager at Blackstone. Sir Patrick was responsible for setting up the MTN & Private Placement Desk and dealer function at Lloyds Bank Plc. He was the first trader for Lloyd's treasury to increase self-led deals significantly from 4% to 32% in 2002.

His journey into content writing has allowed him to become an exceptionally motivated and enthusiastic author and professional communicator.

Sir Patrick is an avid lover of literature. He has published more than 35 books across several genres. How to Trade Derivatives and CFDs To Make Millions, Unlocking the Secrets of Bitcoin & Cryptocurrency Made Easy, Secret of Wealth Creation: Principal lessons on the secrets of building a long-lasting wealth, The future of Cryptocurrency. The Secrets of How to Make Six Figures (and More!), Blockchain And The World of Cryptocurrency, The Blueprint to Intelligent Investors, Intelligent Finance, Private Placement Programs, Beginners of Nowhere, Undying Lust, and Karmic Love are some of his famous works.

Sir Patrick excelled on his journey to become a highly educated and intellectual academic. Aside from being a notable investment banker, he is also currently a professional communicator, author, and philanthropist. His intelligence and educational achievements are evident in his role in multi-national organizations and financial institutions. These include investment banking and a Tier 1 Trader on Wall Street. He has left an impact everywhere he has graced, evident in feedback about him and his work.

Work History and Career

From his humble beginnings at Wells Fargo Bank on wall street, he has served as a private banker, fund manager, and an outstanding bond, futures, and derivatives trader on the trading floors. He established himself in his specialist field in the debt markets and private placement. His financial architecture and creative skills have seen him work with some of the best minds. He is an enigma in his field and founded the MTN & Private Placement Desk at Lloyds Bank PLC.

He has helped large corporations create new credit structures for international supply chains, SMEs for the public sector, private clients, and governments. His innovative and leadership skills have tailored funding and investments for various clients. One of his notable accomplishments was implementing over $1.3 billion in funding for social housing in the Bahamas, and he has gathered a wide range of expertise in venture capital and asset management portfolio. He has backed and advised several successful start-ups while running two significant Funds. His methods are sustainable, and he can boast one of the highest return ratios in the banking sector, assuring clients impressive profits and returns.

Sir Patrick helped create the economic phenomenon of Contract For Difference (CFD), a concept regarded as truly pioneering that today banks and trading institutions now adopt. Using clever leverage ratios, CFD has changed how trading is implemented across capital markets. He has written journals and books about CFD and how to become wealthy by executing his strategies and concepts in wealth creation. He is also a renowned and sought-after wealth manager, managing his trading platform in Private Placement through his desk at Credit Suisse Bank and DBS Bank. He has published several books on Private Placement Programs and Investment trading strategies, all of which have become notable best sellers.

Sir Patrick is a Global Ambassador for the International Rights and Welfare Association (IRAWA) and Ambassador of the Royal Diplomatic Club. In May 2021, he was appointed Ambassador by The Academy of Universal Global Peace USA as a governing board/trustees member and awarded The Human Excellency Award. He is also President of International Banking Relations of the Commonwealth Entrepreneurs Club. He sits as a Trustee and Governor on the board of NGOs and IGOs.

Beliefs

Sir Patrick believes that when people are learning, then they are growing. He is on a quest to make excellence a part of the people he meets. He considers every day as an opportunity to improve the world. He helps people to turn an idea into an opportunity. He teaches how to utilize creative thinking and innovative strategies to become an expert in wealth creation and a humanitarian. He believes no mountain is too high to climb if you have the right tools. Additionally, every obstacle has a solution, and the most challenging dream can be realized with imagination, creativity, and resilience.

CONTENTS

PRIVATE PLACEMENT PROGRAMS

"As my journey continued, I found my mission was evolving. At each stop along the way, I was discovering tools, opportunities, and investment products available to ultrawealthy people that the average person never hears about. And ironically, some of the best ones have very little risk, or they have limited risk with what they call *asymmetric risk / reward* - which means the investors get a big upside potential for very little downside exposure. And that's what the 'smart money' lives for."
- Tony Robbins, pages 25-25, "Money - Master the Game" (#1 New York Times Bestseller)

A SEMINAL FOUNTAIN OF GOOD FOR THE WORLD ECONOMY

In 1933, when the banking cabal had achieved their dream - and the US government declared bankruptcy - the bankers foreclosed on the Washington DC apparatus and took it over more completely than ever before.

House Joint Resolution (HJR) 192 made the labor, the property, and even the bodies of every American the collateral for the so-called "US dollar." But that has two sides to it:

Slave: If people think, as most people do, that their bodies, labor, and property back the money system, then they think they are responsible for the federal debts and taxes, etc. They believe they are the subjects of the state.

Sovereign: But if people realize that - wait a minute, we are the creditors - we are the backing for the money! That makes us the sovereigns in this country. We are the creditors, and the bankers are the debtors.

Exactly like that, there are two ways one can think about Bank Instruments Investment Programs:

Slave: If people think, as most people do, that the Private Placement Platforms trade in debt instruments, and therefore this is "totally evil," - they're thinking in black-and-white duality. They're devolving into "us against them." They're failing to comprehend the intrinsic neutrality of the system and the potential to use its mechanisms for good. They are falling below the system, feeling helpless and powerless to put it to good use.

Sovereign: But if people realize that:
- ❖ The BIIP industry is the only trading market that has no losers on the other side of every trade;
- ❖ It is the largest market on Earth - orders of magnitude larger than Forex;
- ❖ Humanitarian projects that are truly helping the world are being funded by many participants in it;
- ❖ It is the artificial scarcity of money flow that created the illusion of its value, and therefore the abundant distribution of the medium of

exchange powerfully facilitates life-supporting improvements in the world; and

❖ Using it totally for good purposes places one over it instead of under it.

Then they see this as one of the best means to fulfilling the Basel Accords - to transform the world monetary system from a debt-based system to an asset-based system. The generous, humanitarian and philanthropic use of the BIIPs via the PPPs adds to the global money supply, places much of that money into the hands of well-meaning humanitarians, and empowers the improvement of life everywhere.

UNSURPASSED RELATIONSHIPS AT THE APEX OF THE GLOBAL BANK INSTRUMENTS INDUSTRY

We are incredibly fortunate to have become connected with several groups operating at this industry's very apex. They offer benefits not found elsewhere.

We are also associated with several of the finest program administrators in the world. One of our favorites of them has singularly impressive credentials. It is, in fact, a team of people, a consulting group. Their extensive accomplishments in business and government, awards, titles, positions, degrees, humanitarian projects, and other recognitions give them a reputation that makes them an honor to introduce. Their knowledge of international law, connections in worldwide banking, and their mastery of trading processes make the journey smoother and more predictable than other providers.

Naturally, at the minimum, they provide the gold standard, which is not unique to them - namely, absolutely **zero risk**, able to be confirmed by the client before commitment. They provide the highest returns on the planet of any managed funds programs. In the best programs, the programs of choice, returns are **contractually guaranteed** - as predictable as clockwork.

It is a privilege to be invited to participate in their programs, and not all clients are accepted. Contractual terms are only discussed after the trading platform has completed stringent compliance checks to ensure complete adherence to international Anti-Money Laundering laws (AML). An idea of what the newly multiplied wealth will be used for by the client is also taken into consideration. Ideally, the client will have an optimistic worldview that supports humanitarian projects, charities, and causes in tune with natural law. The higher the purpose, the more ideal the client is.

For the entire program duration, the client remains in full control of their committed capital, or its equivalent, at all times, just as is the case now. The cost of doing business is the opportunity cost of that capital just sitting there and not being deployed into other investments. In some reserve account programs, the client is free to move his capital, but if one does, after signing the contract to enter into the program, the returns will stop coming, and the client will probably never be invited to participate again. Nevertheless, that is the worst of it - client funds are never placed at risk. Knowing the outcome is predictable, one can have peace of mind and sleep at night.

This means one doesn't need to do due diligence. One doesn't need to check us out. The client doesn't need to trust us (even though we are trustworthy). It doesn't matter. The client doesn't need to trust the program administrators or the traders. In all but a few programs, the client will never entrust their money with them. The client doesn't need to do due diligence on whether they are trustworthy. The client doesn't need to trust anyone but himself. The client stays in complete control at all times.

That much is already the gold standard, with the few platforms operating with integrity and performing worldwide. What is different about the two firms we represent consists of a number of rare virtues that newcomers and seasoned veterans might have yet to encounter. These rarified values give clients advantages considered rare and privileged even within the elite club of billionaires.

One of these firms operates at the apex of the global financial system, handling the Chinese Heritage Funds and the treasuries of many royal families, among others, which number in the "T" and "Q" levels. This firm sets the policy for all the other platforms and oversees them. So if they can't accomplish something for an investor, nobody can. Its absolute rock bottom minimum for admission into a platform is $500M USD or EUR.

This firm occupies an entire floor of the highest high-rise building in downtown Miami. It has 150 staff and an army of traders, platforms, attorneys, and other professionals in many locations around the world. It is also a prime cutting house, so that is where we refer clients who wish to purchase Bank Guarantees (BGs) or Standby Letters of Credit (SBLCs), as distinguished from entering a bank instruments trading program. There is a $500M USD minimum for purchasing BGs or SBLCs.

Other favored firms have a minimum for participation at only USD 1M or EUR, but they also handle nine, ten, and eleven-figure funds.

We have seen clients and intermediaries being paid regularly, consistently, flawlessly, as promised, and as contractually guaranteed via all of these sources. Hence these platform sources are in that tiny percentage that is proven, genuine, authentic, performing, of integrity, and successful.

Thus we are correct at the quintessence of the global bank instruments industry through two different channels - both of which are heavily involved in humanitarian projects (the genuinely benevolent ones that are truly making a difference for the betterment of the world), both are proven to be performing and paying out as promised, and both of which can authenticate a prospective client on their screens within 15 minutes.

Since programs come and go monthly, for more detailed information regarding the specific programs available from these two firms, see the separate document entitled "Current Programs."

NOTES

_____

_____

_____

_____

_____

_____

_____

_____

_____

_____

_____

_____

_____

_____

_____

NOTES

NOTES

NOTES

NOTES

_____

_____

_____

_____

_____

_____

_____

_____

_____

_____

_____

_____

_____

_____

_____

OVERVIEW

The terms "International Fiduciary Trades," "Private Placement Platforms," and "Bank Instruments Investment Programs" represent a private category of investments that are not available on the open market.

This special type of Trade is part of the process that brings International Bank Instruments from the Primary Market to the Secondary Market, usually involving Medium Term Notes (MTNs).

These are private and by "invitation only" investments from the world's largest and most reputable banks. These are unlike any other investment because the returns are not speculative but are contractual, thereby making them immune to negative public market conditions.

Trading does not take place in the US. Still, it occurs primarily in Europe (London, Zurich, Geneva) and Asia (Hong Kong, Singapore) among top-tier, AAA-rated banks such as JP Morgan Chase, Credit Suisse, Citi Group, HSBC, and others. They generally are only available to Ultra High-Net-Worth Individuals or Qualified Institutional Investors. Because they occur at the upper echelons of the world financial system, they are not available to the general public. For this reason, most Financial Planners and Financial Advisors are not privy to these investments.

The returns can be contractually as high as double-digit monthly returns, and the capital is not put at risk in the trading. With properly structured programs, the Investor's capital always remains in their bank account as the investor acts only as a 3rd party investment partner for the banks.

Banks cannot legally trade their own funds. Therefore, to satisfy the rigid International Banking Regulations that govern this process, the banks must have 3rd party investment funds sitting on their balance sheet at the time of the trades, even though the money is never technically used. Trade proceeds are usually disbursed weekly over 40 weeks (international banking weeks over 12 calendar months).

These are regulated by strict guidelines established by the International Chamber of Commerce (ICC), the Federal Reserve, the European Central Bank, and the Bank of International Settlement (BIS). Both traders and participating financial institutions require special licenses to participate.

A cash investor with sufficient capital can bypass the traditional smaller "Middle Man" Trade Platforms and participate directly with the Bank Trade Desk, receiving a contract on bank letterhead with full banking responsibility. Intermediaries such as a Program Manager and a Facilitator serve to pre-qualify investors, answer their questions, and get all the necessary compliance documents.

The Investor undertakes due diligence once they have submitted KYC (Know Your Client) and POF (Proof of Funds) documents to the Trader and have passed forensic compliance checks. At that point, they will receive the contract from the Trader stipulating the terms and procedures, on bank letterhead, with full banking responsibility. This gives the Investor full transparency and makes due diligence very easy. The serial number of that contract and the banking license of the Trader can easily be verified by the Investor's banker. After reviewing the contract and performing banker due diligence, the Investor decides whether they want to move forward or not.

NOTES

_____

_____

_____

_____

_____

_____

_____

_____

_____

_____

_____

_____

_____

_____

_____

_____

_____

NOTES

NOTES

NOTES

NOTES

BACKGROUND

The "United States Department of the Treasury" (US Treasury), fulfilling its responsibilities under the Bretton Woods Agreement, developed the Medium Term Note (MTN) by employing established European financing methods through which banks and financial institutions commonly finance long-term loans by selling Letters of Credit or Bank Notes of the medium term to provide funding for loans.

The MTN bank issues are debt instruments that are legally allowed to be excluded from the debit side of their ledger or "off-balance sheet" but count towards the bank's capital reserves. Funds received by issuing these instruments rank at an equal rate with depositors' accounts. Still, these are long-term "contractual obligations" and, as such, are allowed to be listed in the footnotes instead of on the balance sheet.

As banks can borrow funds on a leveraged ratio against their capital reserves to engage in fractional reserve lending, this method of financing can be very profitable.

In the post-World War II era, the Bretton Woods Agreement created a stable international financial system and a mechanism to finance macroeconomic projects to rebuild parts of Asia and Western Europe. The US Treasury and the "Federal Reserve System"

(Federal Reserve) developed an instrument that may be traded to create new credit and that credit would be used in specific approved macroeconomic projects, allowing such funds and credit to be applied in geographical areas requiring credit and cash infusions to survive and grow.

While that understanding or intent remains true today, it is no longer always a necessary requirement to involve an economic project / humanitarian project. Investors can engage in either wealth creation or project funding, depending on the client's goal and the terms of the trade program.

The contracts to purchase and sell these MTNs are managed and/or approved by the US Treasury and are administered by prime US and European bank syndicates.

The US Treasury or the Federal Reserve may price these instruments at whatever price is necessary to provide the needed new credit in the geographical location or for the project(s) for which they have been approved.

Not all applicants or projects are approved. The applicant and the funds used to purchase and sell the financial instruments must be screened according to US Patriot Act and Anti-Money Laundering (AML) Guidelines and their European equivalents. Before discussing contract terms, this is done by submitting Know Your Client (KYC) documentation to the Traders, along with Proof of Funds (POF).

Generally, there is just one Principal (or Asset Provider). That Principal is the owner of the Funds, and the Principal is the applicant to the "trade desk," which must also have the approval to trade from the US Treasury or the Federal Reserve.

NOTES

_____

_____

_____

_____

_____

_____

_____

_____

_____

_____

_____

_____

_____

_____

_____

NOTES

NOTES

NOTES

NOTES

NATURE OF THE INVESTMENT

These programs are a very low-risk opportunity for an "Investor" who can provide a cash deposit, Bank Guarantee (BG), or a Standby Letter of Credit (SBLC) for a minimum of 500 Million Euro (€500,000,000), 500 Million USD, or in some rare programs, an absolute minimum of 1 million USD.

This deposit or Bank Instrument (BI) allows the trade bank to release credit facilities for trading MTNs. The notional returns to the Investor/Asset Provider are generally expected to be over 100% per month or per week. This expectation is based on the track record over the last decade. However, returns are contractually agreed upon by the Asset Provider and the Trader before the trading begins and can vary on a case-by-case basis.

For Investors who do not have 500M Euro, there is the possibility to make a wealth-accumulation "bullet trade." These are for Investors with a minimum of 1M Euro or USD, and the trade proceeds are paid weekly to help the Investor get to the 500M Euro level more quickly.

The Investor's capital is not put at risk in the trading. The Investor's capital triggers a credit line for the bank. The bank fully underwrites the credit line before it can be triggered, guaranteeing the Investor's money will never be collateralized.

The Investor's capital is not physically involved (prohibited use) with the buy and resale exchange activities generating the profit. Fiduciary Trade capital always sits in their own bank account, without liability of lien, encumbrance, transfer of control, or subject to first call by anyone, and only serves as a security pledge under contract to a trader.

The trader uses this pledge to trigger his credit facility under contract with his trade bank, which extends a conditional leveraged credit line against the total of his capital contracts with Investors. The bank protects the Investors' account from calls in that the credit facility used to purchase securities is subject to bank-responsible confirmation of a "closed book" sale only.

The trader must have confirmed evidence of contracts with exit buyers (closed book) for the securities before the bank will release the credit line. The bank manages and scrutinizes the sale itself at all times, as their funds and license are exposed.

In other words, the Investor's funds are not directly involved in the buy/resale transactions. The Investor's cash deposit, as a security commitment, is non-callable and not subject to loss liability because of the terms and conditions of the credit line facility in which the transaction resale funds are in place before the release of the credit line.

NOTES

NOTES

_____

_____

_____

_____

_____

_____

_____

_____

_____

_____

_____

_____

_____

_____

_____

NOTES

NOTES

NOTES

MONETIZATION OF ASSETS

For those who have non-cash assets, some firms are ready, able, and willing to obtain lines of credit against them and place that cash into a PPP. All bank instrument traders require USD or EUR as the basic funding unit and do not accept other types of money or assets for trading contracts. In addition, they normally do not accept lines of credit that are already lined or encumbered. They only accept free and clear cash or credit that is unencumbered. However, a few companies arrange for the type of credit against assets that a bank instruments trader can accept.

NOTES

NOTES

_____

_____

_____

_____

_____

_____

_____

_____

_____

_____

_____

_____

_____

_____

_____

_____

_____

NOTES

NOTES

_____

_____

_____

_____

_____

_____

_____

_____

_____

_____

_____

_____

_____

_____

_____

_____

_____

NOTES

HOW TO CONVERT ASSETS FOR SALE INTO PLATFORM TRADE DEALS

Monetizers can bring benefits to many large asset sellers that would be superior to selling the asset by hypothecating it and entering the line of credit into one of our unsurpassed zero-risk pinnacle-of-the-industry bank instruments trading programs in the private placement industry.

This would allow the asset owner to keep ownership of the asset while enjoying the benefits of major cash flow derived from the entry into bank instruments trading programs of the line of credit issued against the asset. This would yield to the asset owner a monthly or weekly series of dollar amounts far greater than a simple one-time sale.

This is a much more favorable and profitable deal for the asset owner, and it is a zero-risk proposal for both the asset owner and the traders. In other words, the asset owner will be able to see in the contract before signing it that their trades never have losses and that even if they did, there would be no legal right for them to claim the asset as reimbursement.

They can never claim ownership of any of the assets, and they can never have any losses on their end. That is why the bank instruments trading industry is kept so quiet. It provides unparalleled privileges to a small private market worldwide by invitation only.

What is necessary to make this happen are just some accessible documents for the asset owner to provide. One of them would be an SKR (Safe Keeping Receipt) from a significant, highly respected financial institution or registered, certified, well-reputed warehouse. That SKR must authenticate the asset's value, ownership, and safety via the standard SKR protocols. The ownership verification will necessarily include the requirement of showing evidence that the chain of title of ownership history is of good, clean, clear, and non-criminal origin.

Once the asset owner passes compliance and is accepted, this will initiate them into the private club of international BIIP PPPs.

NOTES

_____

_____

_____

_____

_____

_____

_____

_____

_____

_____

_____

_____

_____

_____

_____

_____

NOTES

NOTES

_____

_____

_____

_____

_____

_____

_____

_____

_____

_____

_____

_____

_____

_____

_____

_____

NOTES

NOTES

HOW IT WORKS

Besides having unique access to established bank lines-of-credit-successful trade programs require the expertise of qualified licensed traders capable of engaging in the purchase and sale of investment-grade bank debentures in the wholesale market. European regulatory agencies license traders and trades proceed according to strict procedural and legal guidelines. Under present rules, traders cannot use their own assets to trade. This is why third-party investors are necessary.

This trading operation is generally referred to as a "controlled," "managed," or "closed" bank debenture trading effort because the Supply Side of the financial instruments and the Exit Buyer for the financial instruments have already been pre-arranged and the price of the instruments already established. In other words, the licensed traders contractually manage the buy and the re-sale of the financial instruments before any trading actually takes place, thus the term "Managed Buy/Sell."

Therefore, each and every completed trade will result in a net gain (and never a net loss) to the trader. The following procedural protocol is normally followed:

- The investor's funds are never touched (funds verification only).

- Targeted 30% yield per tranche to clients (for example)
- Four tranches a week - with settlements on Friday - there may be multiple trades on a given day.
- No Powers of Attorney.
- No surprises (the Investor/Asset Provider is to be a Signatory to the Buy-Sell Trading Contract).

The crucial distinction, however, is that under a properly managed "buy-sell" transaction, the Investor does NOT transfer any funds to an intermediary escrow attorney or trader, nor are the funds required to be pledged or subjected to a lien.

When moving an MTN into the secondary market through trading,

1. Master Commitment Holders are first in line;
2. Commitment Holders are second in line;
3. The secondary market comes after that.

A bank issues a newly issued or "fresh cut" instrument at a steep discount to face value, for example, 58% of face value. It can only be purchased by a Fed-authorized Master Commitment Holder, who has a quota they must fill annually to keep their Fed appointment.

They line up a number of Commitment Holders with the exclusive right to purchase these MTNs from the Master Commitment Holders, each in smaller volume and at a slight markup. This is the popular business model of "buy wholesale, sell retail" . . . buy wholesale in bulk, then sell in smaller quantities at a higher price.

These Commitment Holders can then sell it as a live seasoned instrument into the secondary market at 98.5% of the face value or similar. The resulting spreads can be substantial. They get contractual commitments from the exit buyers before the initial fresh-cut transaction with the Master Commitment Holder is triggered.

It is all done digitally... authentication, verification, invoicing, and close-out can be done in seconds using Bloomberg or similar.

Again, BIS regulation is that banks cannot sell their authorized issues to each other, which is where the third-party Investor comes in. The Investor is the key for the trader to unlock the credit line from the trade bank.

The traders who do these trades use credit lines from banks, but the credit line has to be fully underwritten before it can be triggered. In other words, the trader must have confirmed evidence of contracts with exit buyers for the MTNs, what they call a "closed book," before the bank releases the credit line. This is risk-free arbitrage . . . the simultaneous purchase and sale of the exact same asset, at the exact same time, but at different prices.

Based on their contractual agreement, the trader keeps a large percentage of that profit and shares the rest with the Investor.

Payouts are usually weekly. Returns are contractually agreed upon by the trader and the Investor based on what paper issues he has lined up. It is usually listed on a minimum or "best efforts" basis. Facilitators can only state "notional double-digit returns per month" and must let the trader disclose to the Investor if it is higher, sometimes as high as 100% per month. Facilitators are not allowed to specify returns, as that is privately contracted between the trader and the Investor after the Investor passes AML compliance.

Because of the high returns, investors with large sums will eventually reach the Wealth Accumulation threshold and will be required to engage in Project Funding, which requires them to donate around 80% of their profits to an economic project (can be as low as 40% or as high as 95%), as non-recourse project funding. However, traders can make more profit per trade if the client engages in project funding. Because of this higher profitability per trade, the net profit to the Investor can be about the same if they do Wealth Accumulation or Project Funding.

The Federal Reserve requires an accounting of those project funds so that they are released only against a certified invoice by the accounting entity. United Nations approval is also necessary for most projects. We have a United Nations Advisor available to fast-track this process.

Experts are also available to assist in helping qualified applicants access PreStructured Humanitarian Projects to fit the precise and rigid guidelines covered by International Banking Law and the United Nations.

NOTES

NOTES

NOTES

NOTES

NOTES

RISKS AND RISK MANAGEMENT

There should be no material risks to the cash deposit or BI, given that the absolute priority is preserving its value and that the BI remains under the control of the Investor at all times.

Since the cash deposit or BI is required to be with a top 25 bank, there is nominal Financial Institution risk should there be a bank bail-in. However, these trade programs only occur among the top 25 banks with AAA credit ratings, which is better than the US Federal Government, and the US Treasury is considered the "risk-free rate."

NOTES

NOTES

NOTES

NOTES

_____

_____

_____

_____

_____

_____

_____

_____

_____

_____

_____

_____

_____

_____

_____

_____

NOTES

INVESTOR FUNDS

Funds have to be of commercial origin, free of any liens or encumbrances. During the term of the Bank Trade, there cannot be any withdrawal of funds from the Client Account, nor shall any loans, credit lines, pledges, hypothecations, liens, or encumbrances be placed against it. The cost of doing business is the opportunity cost of that capital just sitting there, not being deployed into other investments.

Institutional investors such as U.S. pension funds are prohibited under ERISA from purchasing anything that is not on-screen (anything other than live MTNs or registered securities which are screenable). A fresh-cut MTN can only become live or seasoned after its title changes. It receives an ISIN or CUSIP number and is registered for screening on Bloomberg or Reuters.

MTNs pay much higher yields than U.S. treasuries. A 10-year MTN can pay 7% to 8%, whereas the 10-year treasury is only around 2% to 3%, and the MTNs from the top banks have AAA credit ratings, unlike the downgraded credit rating of the U.S. treasuries.

The secondary market is dominated by institutional buyers, like pension funds, sovereigns, and foundations, who buy and hold until maturity while collecting their annual coupon interest. They have to match cash outflows with cash inflows, which is a reliable way for them to do that without the volatility of market speculation in equity markets. These are part of their conservative allocation, while equities and private equity funds are part of their riskier higher-yield allocations.

NOTES

_____

_____

_____

_____

_____

_____

_____

_____

_____

_____

_____

_____

_____

_____

_____

_____

NOTES

NOTES

NOTES

NOTES

WHY THE BIIP INDUSTRY DENIES ITS OWN EXISTENCE

Using the phrase 'Bank Instrument Investment Programs,' in 2019, Google found several top sites (first page of hits), including that of the SEC, to deny that such BIIP programs exist — but not only that the high returns don't exist, but they are outright frauds.

So the first thing that newcomers need to realize is that the only BIIPs to favor are those where the investor never turns over control of his money to anyone else. In the few legitimate programs where the investor does turn over his money to the trader, he must have received a collateral instrument of equal or greater value and liquidity from a reputable institution as recourse. 100% of the scams have been where money changed hands without proper collateral. If the principal capital never changes hands, it is impossible for any BIIP administrator to steal it. Very simple. In the few cases where it does change hands, and a proper collateral instrument is in hand, if the trader fails to return the funds, the investor has only to cash the collateral instrument.

The legitimate programs provide this gold standard of investor control of his principal. He can see well in advance of entering such a program that there is never any requirement to relinquish control of his funds or move them to anyone else's account. And the best BIIPs put no block, no lien, no encumbrance, no assignment, and no added signatory on the funds. All of this an investor can see ahead of time in the communications with the intermediaries, program managers, and in the contract.

This gives peace of mind. It demolishes the claims that all BIIPs are scams. How can a scam even be possible when the principal capital never leaves its owner's control or its equivalent never leaves the investor's possession?

This being the case, then why is the industry allowing itself to be misrepresented like this by the government and official financial websites and publications?

The reason is crystal clear. It is a private club. It is elitist. It is an inner circle. It is not exactly "secret," but it is very much low-key and "quiet". It has to be, because if it were allowed to be publicly broadcast, can you imagine the turmoil and implosion effects it would have on the world economy? Billions and trillions of dollars would pour out of the high-risk stock and bond markets and even real estate, and into the BIIPs. And let's face it, the instruments traded in the BIIPs are based on these other markets. So if it were to allow itself to be too well known, and to be widely endorsed, it would end up sabotaging itself by collapsing the very markets on which its instruments are derived. Therefore, it has been mandatory for the industry to surround itself with a smokescreen of self-denial. Only the privileged few who are somehow fortunate enough to be initiated into it know the true reality of it.

An interesting story illustrates all this. A former three-term California State Senator and prominent American attorney had his principal offices in Geneva, Switzerland, and Sacramento, California, and served as Chairman of the Board or CEO of several corporations. He had satellite offices in London, England; Melbourne, Australia; San Jose, Costa Rica; Shenyang, China; Johannesburg, South Africa; and Trivandrum, India. As a result of his expertise in global matters, he also served as an international advisor to the California State University School of Business & Economics.

During his three terms as Senator, he was Chairman of the Senate Judiciary Committee, the Business and Professions Committee, vice-chairman of the Public Utilities and Energy Committee, and a member of the Senate Finance and Banking and Commerce Committees.

Without divulging his name to protect his privacy, it is important merely to realize that someone with these credentials and accomplishments became a believer and participant in the BIIPs. But it was not always that way. It all started when a wealthy Middle Eastern oil family approached him in Switzerland.

They informed him that they were committing some very large funds to a special private program that contractually promised they would stay in control of their principal capital and never relinquish it to anyone else. All they wanted the former Senator to do was to study the contracts and confirm that this freedom from risk really was true. They wanted to avoid being tricked. They wanted absolute confirmation that the absence of risk was real, and they were willing to pay generously for this advice.

When he saw that they were getting into a BIIP, he informed them that "no such programs exist." He informed them that it had to be a scam somehow. But they countered with a bold assertion that they were not seeking his opinion on the program's reality or legitimacy. They were only retaining him to perform one thing: to ensure their capital would never be at risk. They did not care about his personal opinion of whether the program was valid. And they were offering a large retainer fee to him for this service.

Therefore, he agreed, still arguing that the program wasn't real. As a condition for his service, he required that he be given access to view the screens showing their funds AND the returns - if any - on the investment. They agreed. Thus, he first fulfilled his commitment to ensuring their funds would never be at risk. He analyzed all the arrangements and became satisfied with them. Hence, they entered the program, and the trading commenced.

Lo and behold - the returns began materializing. He could see them coming in on the bank screens. The returns quickly exceeded the amount of the principal, thus demonstrating that there had to be a genuine huge source of profits somewhere. He was shocked. Furthermore, he was paid what he called - in his words - "a rather princely sum" - for his asset protection legal services.

This initiated him into the BIIP industry. He then became an enthusiastic supporter of it. He became a principal participant in it with his own money and a facilitator for other investors. He then clearly understood why he had previously bought into the public party line about the nonexistence of the programs. He understood the need to keep it quiet.

Newcomers also often want to see or hear of a testimonial of someone who has already made the high returns claimed. Testimonials exist, but only if the newcomer happens to know someone who has experienced a genuine BIIP or at least knows someone who knows someone. It goes without saying that BIIPs cannot be advertised because that would violate the "keep it quiet" mandate. Since they cannot be advertised, offering testimonials from satisfied customers would also be out of the question.

Since the industry is so highly profitable for the insiders who are in it, it is rare that it ever needs to seek newcomers to come in and provide their capital on the books, based on which new credit is issued, which is used in the trading. With this being the case, the newcomers need the BIIP administrators - not the other way around. The BIIP program managers don't "need" new investors. That is why all legitimate BIIPs state that they are "by invitation only".

So, newcomers with the "prove it to me" attitude only amuse the insiders. They are left behind to live in their own skepticism and are deprived of the benefits of the BIIP.

Thus you can see that the entire industry operates by word of mouth. It operates by someone knowing someone who privately informs someone. Those who have this good fortune can get initiated into it, but if they have the "prove it to me" attitude, they will be passed up. They are not needed.

Two things ameliorate the requisite amount of faith in the reality of a BIIP that is therefore required for a newcomer to be open to it:

1. the proven-up-front absence of any risk to his principal capital; and
2. hopefully, personal acquaintance with someone who can vouch for the program's performance.

At least the first source of confidence is always available in any real BIIP. The second depends upon each newcomer's personal relationships. In the absence of that, he has to give it a try and see for himself if the performance manifests.

NOTES

NOTES

NOTES

NOTES

NOTES

DISPELLING MYTHS ABOUT BANK INSTRUMENTS

There is so much misinformation in the Bank Guarantee and Standby Letter of Credit industry, largely because there is a huge vacuum of information.

Banks don't Issue Bank Guarantees and Standby Letters - the bank is the deliverer, not the initiator of the transaction.

Banks operate exactly the same way with Bank Guarantees and Standby Letters of Credit. The Bank is the Post Office, and they receive financial instruction from a Provider to deliver one of the Provider's assets (BG or SBLC) to the specific address of the Receiver.

The Bank is just the delivery boy who works for the BG & SBLC Provider. The Provider is the actual asset owner, asset holder, and asset controller.

Most clients incorrectly think the Bank is the Provider who initiates and completes the delivery of the Bank Guarantee or Standby Letter of Credit. This is 100% NOT TRUE!

Banks never initiate a Bank Guarantee or Standby Letter of Credit Transaction.....

NEVER! The Bank is simply the Postman who works for the Asset owner / Provider.

So who are BG & SBLC Providers?

BG & SBLC Providers are high net worth corporations or individuals who hold bank accounts at the issuing bank that contain significant cash sums. The BG or SBLC Provider instructs his issuing bank to secure and encumber cash in his own account and authorizes the bank to create a financial instrument, e.g., a Bank Guarantee or Standby Letter of Credit, and deliver that financial instrument by Swift to the Receiver's bank account with which the Provider has contracted.

The Bank has no interest in the transaction apart from receiving fees for "cutting" (creating) the financial instrument and "delivering" the financial instrument. All other responsibility for the asset is the Provider's because the financial instrument was created and is secured against the cash position in the Provider's own bank account at the issuing bank.

Banks don't use BGs or SBLCs to raise Capital because if a Bank wants to raise Capital (e.g., take in more money to grow), the bank issues Bank Stock or Shares, Bank Bonds, or MTNs (Mid Term Notes).

BGs or SBLCs are secured against client cash accounts of the Provider in the Bank. The Bank NEVER uses its own cash to encumber or secure a BG or SBLC!

When was the last time you saw a Bank advertising Monetizable Bank Guarantees or Standby Letters of Credit for sale? Answer: Never! Why? Because BGs and SBLCs are not bank products, they are niche market client products created at the request of high-net-worth bank clients with large cash holdings at the bank.

Go to your local Bank Branch and tell the Bank Officer at the branch that you want to buy or Lease a

Bank Guarantee. Most won't know what you are talking about because BGs and SBLC are NOT publicly offered Bank products.

To issue a BG or SBLC, you need to have a special bank account called a custodial account. A custodial account is a special bank account that can hold, issue and receive financial instruments. It takes 3 months+ to establish a custodial account at a bank.

There are very few genuine BG or SBLC Providers. Issuing BGs & SBLC requires a very specialized financial skill set, and most High Net worth Investors don't have the time, patience, expertise, or desire to involve themselves with BG and SBLC Issuing.

The fact is you need the BG & SBLC Provider much MORE than they need YOU! A Genuine Provider has more clients than they need, so they are VERY selective about with whom they choose to do business!

If you want more education on this topic, you can read books like "Bank Guarantees in International Trade: The Law and Practice of Independent (First Demand) Guarantees and Standby Letters of Credit in Civil Law and Common Law Jurisdictions", by R. Bertrams; or "Letters of Credit and Bank Guarantees under International Trade Law" by Matti S. Kurkela.

NOTES

NOTES

_____

_____

_____

_____

_____

_____

_____

_____

_____

_____

_____

_____

_____

_____

_____

_____

NOTES

NOTES

NOTES

DON'T BE DECEIVED BY BROKER JOKERS

Sometimes genuine clients with real money don't find us - or if they hear about us from one of our intermediaries, they aren't given correct information - and so they go away. That is a tragedy.

On the other hand, sometimes they go away, not because one of us has misinformed them, but because they were misinformed by other brokers representing other schemes. Unfortunately, the majority of would-be intermediaries out there are not connected with real platforms with real-performing programs. They think they are - but their "connection" is only another broker - who may be claiming to be the source.

From these phonies, investors hear rumors like the following:

Rumor: You can pay a small amount to lease a BG and enter it into a trading program.

Fact: Legitimate platforms only allow owned instruments, not leased ones. Or if it is leased, the signed permission of the owner is required to put it into the trade.

Rumor: You can get into a "funds don't move" platform with small-cap money.

Fact: "Funds don't move" programs are only available at 100M+. (However, at least one program does exist with a minimum entry of £ 1M in which funds do have to move, but only to a new non-depletion account in his own name and control at a top bank in Europe.)

A common problem in the BIIP industry is that for every genuine platform that is truly performing, and where no client ever loses any money, there are a thousand others that are rumored to exist - but don't exist at all.

These rumors are spread by brokers who don't have a direct connection with a genuine trading platform. They only have connections with other intermediaries, many of whom claim to be the platform. Their motive for exaggerating is often to attract real money and then hope to place it successfully somewhere.

When one broker successfully copies information heard from another broker, it gets passed to another broker and then another and another. That is called a "daisy chain". It is a sad fact that most brokers out there are like this. They have never had direct contact with a genuine and performing platform. They only think they do, but they have never verified it.

Then when genuine investors produce real POF (Proof of Funds), the broker sends it up the line, and it ends up getting circulated through dozens of people, ending nowhere. It never leads to a genuine deal. In some unfortunate cases, it ends up in the hands of a scamster. But more often, it just generates a lot of busy activity among a lot of people and delivers no joy to the investor or anyone. Just frustration and disappointment.

This has made a bad name to the industry. It is a symptom of the fact that the industry must remain private. Otherwise, it could widely broadcast the truth about the situation to the general public. In the vacuum, in the absence of the truth being widely broadcast, it is understandable that the field would be rife with false rumors.

NOTES

NOTES

NOTES

NOTES

NOTES

WHY DO BANKS ISSUE MTNS?

Banks issue MTNs because they can leverage the funds 10:1 and loan it out at interest for 10 years, turning a hefty profit. Below is an illustrative example...

1. Full Face Value of MTN Issue (FFV): 10 Billion Euro
2. Sell at 58% of Face Value: 5.8 Billion Euro
3. Coupon value at 7.5% per annum: 7.5 Billion Euro
4. Liability (Point 2 - {1+3}): 11.7 Billion Euro
5. Leverage at 10:1: 58 Billion Euro
6. Interest by bank at 3% per annum on Point 5: 17.4 Billion Euro 7: Profit made by Bank (Point 4+6): 5.7 Billion Euro

NOTES

NOTES

_____

_____

_____

_____

_____

_____

_____

_____

_____

_____

_____

_____

_____

_____

_____

_____

NOTES

NOTES

NOTES

COSTS

The Asset Provider is not required to make any upfront fee payments.

Typical Platform fees would be around 10% (lawyers and attorneys) and are paid from the profit disbursement from that tranche. (See Q & A for an example of profit disbursement).

Because these are International Fiduciary Trades, made by invitation only, under strict non-solicitation rules, it is customary to have facilitating intermediaries involved in the introduction. Those intermediaries are compensated with a small referral fee of 5%, usually paid out of the trading profits by the Paymaster, before net profits are distributed to the Asset Provider.

The person who introduced you to these programs may have humanitarian projects or life-supporting businesses they wish to fund. In these cases, a percentage profit share from your returns can be negotiated for this purpose prior to introductions being made. Since returns are so high and are unattainable in any other managed investment, especially at zero risk, a share of somewhere in the region of 30% to 50% is usually agreed upon, but this is a private negotiation between the investor and the introducer.

It is important for you to know that the platforms strictly do not allow pre-arranged side agreements for profit sharing with outside parties. Therefore, this type of agreement is best conducted within a single entity, such as a trust or corporation.

This way, the trust or corporation is the 'single client' applying for the platform trading account, with you and your profit-sharing introducer as co-signatories on the entity. The platform is then only responsible for paying out to this single entity and can do the necessary KYC checks on both parties.

Once the entity is paid, then you and your partner can distribute the proceeds internally, according to your mutual agreement.

NOTES

NOTES

NOTES

NOTES

NOTES

HOW TO PROTECT YOURSELF IN PPP PROGRAMS

Private Placement Platform Programs (PPPs) are one of the most misunderstood of all the Alternative Investments. Due to the enormous amount of misleading, false and fake information floating around the internet, as well as the fact there are very few published sources of quality information, we have created a quick and simple guide that will allow you, in seconds, to differentiate a legitimate Private Placement Program from a scam.

Every scam needs a mechanism to move money from the client into the scammer's pocket. If that mechanism is not present, then the scam, by definition, cannot work.

There are two main mechanisms scammers use in PPP scams that are not present in legitimate deals. The reason they use these two approaches is because it is the only way for them to gain access to a client's money in the deal. In the vast majority of cases, articles and stories where people tell you about scams, one of these two mechanisms is always present. It is, in fact, the only thing that allows the scam to work.

1. Up-front fees: Traditional Legitimate Private Placements DO NOT have Up-Front Processing Fees. This is a simple little money transfer mechanism that gets you to pay money for services you're never going to receive.

2. 3rd Party Accounts: This is the most predominant scam technique in the industry. It is a way for scammers to gain access to large amounts of funds, by having the investor move the funds to a less secure 3rd party or 3rd party escrow account where they can easily access and steal it.

In a Traditional Private Placement Program, the money stays in your own AAA Rated Top-Tier Bank Account, in your name. In most cases it is held in place by the Bank itself for the duration of the trade program. No one else has access to the funds, ever. The trade contracts are done with the banks, on bank letter head with fullbanking responsibility, and these contracts have verifiable bank serial numbers so that your banker can do bank-to-bank verification for you.

There are also very strict Non-Solicitation Laws enforced for these, per International Banking Law. Seeing any type of advertising for these services online or sharing program details on a website, a blog, or a video is a breach of those solicitation laws and is highly illegal. This is one of the easiest ways to spot scams immediately.

Now let's talk about Legitimate Private Placement Programs. These are done by word-of-mouth only, through intermediaries with pre-existing relationships, generally by people with very substantial and easily verifiable credentials. In presenting this information to potential clients, they are staking the reputation that many of them worked a lifetime to establish. That is a good starting point because the program they are discussing with you is legitimate.

Next, since there are NO upfront fees and the money never leaves the client's AAA Rated bank account, you have to ask yourself in a Properly Structured deal, "If the money is in my Bank Account, and there are no upfront fees, no third-party accounts, and there are verifiable Bank Contracts if you were a scammer, how exactly would you make any money doing this?" Of course, the answer is that you wouldn't.

Since the contracts are with AAA Rated Banks, the Investor Client is covered by the same protections that govern the bank. This means that if there is a problem with the contract, the bank can be held liable under the law and potentially lose its banking license.

Next, there are Insurance Wraps from AAA-rated Insurance firms, like Lloyd's of London, in the 100s of millions of dollars available for personal protection on these deals and to wrap hard assets for the trades themselves. An AAA-rated Insurance company would do business with a bank trade desk risking money daily in these amounts, which is a solid indication you have found a legitimate bank trade desk.

The hang-up that most Investor Clients have is that the Bank requires anti-money laundering (AML) Compliance and a thorough background check before a potential investor can be introduced to the little-known bank departments that handle these. You may only have 20 people in the entire network of the bank that know these departments even exist. One of the main reasons for this is that the banks want their employees, including upper management, to do their regular jobs instead of chasing down clients for Managed Buy/Sell programs, earning millions in intermediary fees, and quitting or retiring.

The banks can lose their license if caught talking to criminals about these programs. Therefore, true due diligence and competition for transparency with the bank and all parties involved can only be achieved after AML compliance documents have been submitted and reviewed.

This report is the extent of the due diligence that can be achieved beforehand. After passing compliance, however, thorough due diligence is very easy. Unfortunately, because of the numerous scams, you can now easily spot, nearly every Private Placement Program gets written off as a scam, and many people need to learn what is truly one of the safest and most profitable Alternative Investments in existence when structured properly.

The bottom line is that every investment class has numerous scams as well as fantastic opportunities. Being educated in how the scams work is your best protection if you wish to enjoy the benefits of working with legitimate bank trade desks that have been quietly doing business for decades.

NOTES

NOTES

NOTES

NOTES

NOTES

QUESTIONS AND ANSWERS

Q: I know it says there is no risk, however, the investors are providing sensitive information about themselves and their accounts. Is there any risk of identity fraud? Who actually sees the information that they provide?

A: This is a good question that some others have asked. It is appreciated that less professional brokers of PPPs have been known to shop investor paperwork around, looking for acceptance at a platform. Then the investor starts receiving calls from unknown parties who have received his private information. Naturally, this would be very unsettling. Thus, please consider the following points.

1. The first thing to realize is that absolute privacy is already nonexistent before even coming to us. Credit data on just about everyone with a credit history is already available on the dark underground net. Intelligence agencies already have everything about everyone in real-time. Any money of any significant size is already showing on screens, along with everything about its owner.

2. Reputable consultants do not shop investor KYC forms. They submit them only and exclusively to the one place where they belong: the trading desk.

3. The most sensitive information is not requested in the initial intake documents. That is only requested later, after the contract is signed, and it only goes directly to the trader. It is never needed by the compliance officer or the intermediaries.

4. Most owners of substantial capital, such as $10 million or more, know they should never deposit it at a bank's ordinary street retail level, facilitated by the lowest-paid bank clerks. That raises a small risk of fraud and attempted theft by such employees. Rather, most high-net-worth owners of capital do their banking at higher levels of the institution, typically called private banking, where much more significant security is routine.

5. In the PPPs, since the cash deposit or BI is required to be with a top-25 bank, there is nominal Financial Institution risk. These trade programs only occur among the top 25 banks with AAA credit ratings, which is better than the US Federal Government, and the US Treasury is considered to be the "risk-free rate". In addition, our recommended PPPs ONLY operate on Tier 1 platforms - meaning we deal directly and only with the 'highest of the high-level traders. Not only are they of the highest integrity, but they also have the greatest proven credibility and reputation in the industry. They stand to gain endlessly more success by continuing to honor their client's rights, and they have the most to lose by not doing so.

6. It is suggested to obtain and use a Protonmail email address. Protonmail has the most invulnerable email encryption in the world and protects email attachments as well, but only if the email is between one Protonmail user and another. The link to obtain your own account is https://protonmail.ch/invite.

Q: Have you seen one of these investments completed?

A: In a word, yes. References of satisfied customers are not allowed due to privacy, confidentiality, and nondisclosure, but we have seen the successful completion of these program payouts since the 1990s, including currently and presently. So YES, clients are now getting paid, and the cash flows.

Q: Can you please clarify the difference between Bullet Trade and 40 Week trade?

A: A bullet trade is a lump sum payment, one time. A 40-week trade goes for 40 weeks and is usually paid weekly or biweekly. Bullet trades only become available a few times per year. Some pay in 24 hours, some pay in 10 days, and some have a 40- week contract that goes with them. It may pay a lump sum payment in a few days or weeks, after which the proceeds can be added to the capital committed to the program for a 40-week contract. Keep in mind that the details of deals change every week, so it is impossible to predict exactly what kind of deal your investors will get in advance. Generally, the larger the investor's capital, the more choices he/she will be given.

Q: It says, "Qualifying Banks: Top-rated international bank preferred". Is there a site I can reference for a list of preferred banks?

A: Yes. There is a list of acceptable banks at this link:https://risk.lexisnexis.com/insights-resources/article/bank-rankings-top-banks-in-the-world

Q: Once everything is set up and executed, how long will the Investor start seeing distribution deposits?

A: It varies from account to account. If the investor puts in $100M or more, it can be pretty quick, like within one week. It is generally under one month if he puts in less than $100M.

Q: Is it possible to bring multiple people together (via an LLC, Inc, etc...) to create the $1M+ minimum needed to participate? Advice on how to do so, if possible?

A: The possibility of this is more answered on your side than on the trading team's side. The reason for this is that, no, the trade programs do not allow pools. They also do not allow borrowed funds. So a group of investors could be assembled, and their funds could be pooled in an LLC or corporation, but it would be illegal to inform them that their money is going into a BIIP. It would be illegal to advertise it. It would be illegal to tell them that their principal capital is guaranteed or that the returns are guaranteed. This is because the trading platform does not accept pools and will not be responsible to multiple parties. Therefore, what investor would put up any money under conditions like that? "We can't tell you what your money is being invested in, and we can't promise any guarantees on it." Nobody would be interested in a deal like that. One LLC director or corporate president can serve as the signatory on the funds in that corporation, but remember, the trading platform requires proof of the history of funds - where the funds came from. If it is revealed that the funds came from smaller contributors who are expecting a return, the fund will be rejected. Only a single lump sum of capital controlled by a single signatory, or a maximum of two signatories, is permitted.

Q: It mentions under "Terms," there is an attached spreadsheet. I did not see one. Can you please resend it?

A: That's because the table in the spreadsheet was converted to a chart and was included in the text herein, inter alia.

Q: After you enter a 40-week trade, can the investor stop it and pull all money if need to, OR is it "once it starts, there is no stopping until 40 weeks"?

A: Yes, the investor can stop at any time. He can remove his capital at any time. If he does, of course, the returns will stop, and most likely, he will never be invited again in the future to participate unless he had a really good reason for terminating, such as some major disaster beyond his control, creating an emergency that merited the urgent need for the funds.

Q: May Russian citizens participate? If yes, may they keep money in a Russian bank?

A: Russians may participate, and if they have over 100M in Sberbank, there is a platform that can work with that. We've never heard of any other Russian banks being accepted, though.

Q: Are there any countries where their citizens are excluded?

A: North Korea and Iran are excluded from participating in these trade programs, as are their citizens.

Q: I understand that the investor could be either a company or an individual. Are there any requirements for the company?

A: The company can be a C-Corp or LLC or Trust or Foundation . . . as long as they have a Board Resolution appointing the signatory on the bank account to represent the company, as worded in the Corporate KYC template, that is fine.

Q: How much in commissions do intermediaries receive?

A: Typically, intermediaries receive a total of 5%, which is split between them. Intermediary fees are usually paid out of the gross trade proceeds, not the client's net, depending on the terms agreed upon for that specific program. On large-cap deals, the percentage is lower.

Q: Is there any agreement that we will be signed between us and/or my associates or any other documents as far as an Intermediary is concerned?

A: Intermediaries get signed into the deal that the investor-client agrees to with the trading team. First, the intermediary introduces and lets the client submit his KYC intake documents. Then if he is approved and invited, all intermediaries will be brought into the documentation at that point.

Q: Who might the Master Commitment Holders be, for example, if known?

A: Some other clients with 500M+ invested.

Q: Who might the Commitment Holders be, for example, if known?

A: Some other clients with 100M+ Invested

Q: What number is the Client/Investor in the payment order?

A: Typically, trading occurs Mondays through Thursdays. They adjudicate on Friday, and the Transaction Paymaster pays everyone at the same time.

Q: What is the secondary market?

A:https://www.investopedia.com/terms/s/second arymarket.asp The secondary market is the public market. For stocks in the USA, that's the NYSE, and companies have to IPO on the NYSE. For Medium Term Notes, Euroclear lists the MTN in the secondary (public) market.

Q: Is the secondary market such as 401-K funds, mutual funds, organization funds, Insurance Investment funds, or other (please specify)?

A: Anybody with enough money can buy MTNs listed on Euroclear.

Q: Can an intermediary be a trust, or must it be an individual with the commissions paid to his trust?

A: An individual, trust, or corporate entity is fine.

Q: What restrictions or requirements are placed on the Intermediaries?

A: Intermediaries are not part of the NDA nor the Contract / Investment Agreement and, as such, are not supposed to know the details of the contract, but if they do, they're still not supposed to disclose it. An intermediary can discreetly show payment of their intermediary fee since they are not part of the NDA, but they cannot disclose the name of the Platform or the Client/Investor.

Q: Would you be able to provide an example of the distribution of a possible tranche?

A: Master Commitment Holders and Commitment Holders are Investors/Clients. If trading is on a 'best efforts basis, then the Platform/Trader usually splits the GROSS trading profits with the Investor/Client 50/50, then the Investor/Client pays any fees out of their gross 50%. Total profit distribution per tranche: 50% to Platform/Trader, 50% to Investor/Client. Of the 50% GROSS to Investor/Client, the Investor/Client NETs 85% of that (85% NET) because of the typical fees of 10% PPA for Platform Fees (bankers and attorneys) and 5% to Intermediaries. However, when the Investment Agreement lists a contractual return, the Platform/Trader pays the Investor/Client the stipulated amount. It keeps the rest, regardless of what the Gross trading profits per tranche were, and then the Investor/Client pays the 10% PPA and 5% intermediary fee as usual.

Q: Is the intermediary's commission percentage based upon the trade total, for example, 5%?

A: It is based on the profit payout to the investor client. If it is a standard 40-week trade contract, the platform usually pays the intermediary commissions, especially in large-cap deals.

Q: My understanding is that Banks and traders are not allowed to trade their own funds. So how can the bank be a party to the such a contractual agreement?"

A: Included in the agreement is the ability of the bank to monitor the client's balance to ensure that the client has not moved the principal capital that he has promised to leave in the account during the term of the contract. As you know, this does not give the bank access to the funds, but it does give the bank access to the information about how much is in the account - and whether the principal that the client agreed to leave in there is still there.

This has traditionally been accomplished via the so-called "tear sheet," - a term from the old days when paper used to be written on. Today, of course, it is all done by computers. More recently, our currently favored compounding trade program, which is available for all levels of investors from £ 1M up, does not use the tear sheet method. Instead, it monitors the client's balance internally; but whatever the method, the end result is the same. The traders must be able to see that the client's principal is still there. That is what is meant by "it can be verified on bank to bank basis by the client's banker".

Q: How can the bank be liable for non-performance?

A: In the favored programs, non-performance has never happened. If non-performance were to happen within an agreed-upon span of time, then the contract stipulates that the client is released from the contract and it is terminated. Although this provision is in any good trading contract, it has never been triggered in the favored programs, fortunately.

This means the worst case scenario might be a waste of some time . . . a few weeks, a month, etc., waiting for the performance, and then the termination of the contract if the performance doesn't happen. But as stated inter alia, this has never happened with the platforms of choice.

Q: Can a hard asset be used in place of cash? Let s say the hard asset is a private residence valued at $1 million+. Could this be done, and if so, what would the procedures be, and what is the approximate LTV for the credit line?

A: No BIIP platform on the planet accepts anything but cash in USD or EUR, or in a few cases, GBP. Administrators who say they accept other things are not the actual platform admin. Rather, they have outside arrangements with monetizers, who then connect the line of credit with the platform.

All investors who have assets in other forms must liquidate those assets first. Borrowed capital is acceptable if it does not have a lien or encumbrance against it. This rules-out mortgages. It is rare for anyone to have borrowed capital of the size required for free and clear platforms of any liens or encumbrances.

Thus, someone with real estate, which is their only source of cash, would have no choice but to sell the real estate and then place the cash proceeds into the platform. With unsurpassed returns and zero risk, the BIIPs available through the platforms are by far the best investments in the world. The price one has to pay to get into them is to come up with the required level of cash - clean, unencumbered, free and clear, of non-criminal origin - and a nice, respectful, cooperative attitude.

Related Question: If a prospective client has real estate, can a trade desk issue credit against that for trading, especially if the real estate is free and clear?

Answer: It makes no difference to the trading platform. They're not concerned with the collateral. Only the lender is. If it is free and clear and someone takes out a loan against it, the lender will be happy that he will have the only lien position on the property. And he can loan more against the equity if the equity is 100%.

But as to the trading platform, that is irrelevant. To help you understand this clearly, remember that investor funds are never traded. Only lines of credit are traded. Credit cannot be issued against credit. See? If it is a mortgage, like a loan from a bank or a public financial institution, it is registered in the banking system as a credit against real estate. Credit cannot be issued against credit. Credit can only be issued against an asset - such as free and clear cash, real estate equity, etc.

And, the trade desks have elected not to get into monetizing real estate. That in itself is a huge, complicated business that requires lots of expertise, licenses, regulations, etc. That's why whole financial institutions are dedicated to it. BIIP traders are usually small teams. They command huge amounts of money, but they are small numbers of people. And they are private, as you know. They do not operate in the public sector as institutional lenders do. That is why private placement platforms don't get into monetizing and making loans. The client has to come with cash or a cash-backed bank instrument. Then the trader's bank can issue credit against the cash or against a cash-backed bank instrument but nothing else.

Now, if the owner of the real estate has a friend, a family member, or some business contact who is willing to issue a private loan, not as a financial institution and not as a bank, but as a private lender, where the money will show up in the borrower's account as if it is his - and if it doesn't show up on the radar of the banking system - then it is considered to be real money by the trading desk. They can issue their credit against it for trading. See? The private lender can record a lien against the real estate at the county recorder as a security on his loan. However, it's still okay - because it's not a bank loan or a financial institution loan showing up in the interbank computer system. That is acceptable to PPP trade desks. I hope this clarifies.

Q: May a public company be a client for PPP? Would it not be considered collecting money from many people?

A: The public company can be a client for a PPP, but the CEO and/or executive management empowered as signatories for the corporation would be under a nondisclosure agreement. In fact, all clients of any kind from anywhere, with any organization, or as individuals, are all under nondisclosure about it.

This means a public company must not disclose exactly from where the new money has come. All they can say are vague sources like "investments", "banking", "consulting", "sales profits", or things like that. It is not allowed to say "bank instruments platform", because it is not a public market. It is a private market, and it wants its existence kept quiet.

Further, the executive management of the company needs to wait to get the permission of the shareholders before placing funds in the platform. The executive management have the discretion to use company funds for investment in whatever they feel will benefit the company. Of course, they are held responsible for the results, but no one will complain if the company profits from its actions.

A story will illustrate this. Chrysler corporation was failing and heading towards bankruptcy in 1979. The CEO at that time, Lee Iacocca, secured $1.5 billion in government loan guarantees. But that was not enough to turn Chrysler around quickly. How were the loans to be repaid?

Miraculously, in just a year or so, everyone was like, "Wow! How did you do it?" Article after article was published, marveling at how it was done.

Iacocca wrote two words in his book which hinted at what he did. He said he was able to turn Chrysler around and repay the loans by investing in "banking programs". He almost blew the lid on it. Back then, nondisclosure agreements were not as strict as they are today. But this gives you an example of how a public company was able to participate in a PPP and benefit the world thereby.

Q: The same question exists for a private company. May it be a client for the PPP if it has several investors?

A: Investing pools made up of multiple smaller investors are not allowed in the platforms. Therefore the company must apply as a single entity with one or two authorized signatories. Like with the public company, those signatories are not allowed to spill the beans about exactly what they are investing in and how they are profiting so handsomely. If they do, they will be removed immediately from the program and will be blacklisted from ever participating again in ANY BIIP worldwide.

Q: Does a company have to be long established, or can a new company be a client in a PPP?

A: When it comes to the likelihood of acceptance to the bank instruments trading platform, being new or long-established doesn't matter. What matters for getting accepted are things like:

- ❖ Do they have the sufficient capital?
- ❖ Is the capital liquid and unencumbered?
- ❖ Does the capital's history of derivation indicate that it is clean, clear, and of noncriminal origin?
- ❖ Is the owner or authorized signatory clean or blacklisted?

All of these things will be determined quickly by the platform's compliance officers as soon as the client has submitted the KYC and POF file. How long the company has been in business is of no concern to them.

Q: Do any platforms accept bonds for trade? I have one potential client with 1 Billion in Sovereign Bonds. I have another potential client who has a 350M USD corporate bond.

A: The answer is yes and no. We will start with the "no" so the "yes" will be clearer.

Please understand that no legitimate and authentic working and performing bank instruments trading platform on the planet accept anything but cash USD or cash EUR. No other assets. When we say "cash", of course, we don't mean physical currency. We mean United States Dollars in a bank account or Euro Dollars in a bank account. No real estate, gold, oil, SBLCs, BGs, bonds, non-cash assets, and not even Swiss Francs or Japanese Yen.

They only work with USD or EUR. Period. That's it. 100%. That's the ONLY thing they accept. Cash is king. Please keep that in mind. Anyone who tells you otherwise is telling you a story. Of course, if the client has capital in a major currency that is traded on the

Forex, other than USD or EUR, the platform might accept it, but only because it is instantly convertible to USD or EUR. The trades are only conducted in USD or EUR.

But the "yes" comes from collaborations with monetizers that are not the same as, but that are connected with, the platforms. Nevertheless, our question to the owners of the bonds is, why don't you sell them and put the cash into a BIIP PPP? You'll make a lot more money doing that than holding on to them. It is slower and more complicated to monetize them.

As often happens, a lot of stuff gets presented to platform consultants because the purveyors have something worthless that they couldn't get value from anywhere else. Their bonds are so exotic, or their other instruments are so questionable that no bank will touch them, and no legitimate monetizer or platform will touch them either. So they go shopping it around. It wastes a lot of time. If the owner could get their instrument monetized successfully, that means they could also get it outright sold. And if he can't sell it, it may be unlikely he could get a line of credit against it, too.

Nevertheless, there are several genuine and major sources for the monetization of assets. Their minimum value for consideration is 150M. It cannot be known whether the actual instruments qualify until they are analyzed. But at least if the asset's appraised value is at least USD 150M, it can be considered.

Naturally, lots of questions would arise. For example, on the sovereign bonds, how old? How recent? And which country? Monetizers consider all these things and more.

Q: Can leased bank instruments be placed into the trade?

A: Previously, we have written that BGs, MTNs, and SBLCs that are leased are not permitted for entry into BIIPs on the PPPs. However, further discussions have illustrated the need to unpack that concept and bring it more into focus.

Leased instruments cannot be placed into trading if the signatory on it is the lessee. It would be great to find a way for that to happen. However, the ledger cannot be transferred. Therefore, it cannot be blocked and traded. Alternatively, suppose the asset holder (the entity holding the actual cash) is willing to issue an instrument without any liens or encumbrances and have the client become the beneficiary. In that case, there could be an opportunity.

A leased Instrument can be traded, but 95% of the time, it isn't because the owner will not issue a block 760, 799, or even an MT542. It is usually leased for credit enhancement only. Unless the asset holder joins in the trade with the client (lessee), they will not release or block the instrument for use.

FOR INFORMATIONAL PURPOSES ONLY As Covered Under International Chamber of Commerce (ICC) Uniform Customs and Practice for Documentary Credits (UCP 600)

NOTES

NOTES

NOTES

NOTES

NOTES

_____

_____

_____

_____

_____

_____

_____

_____

_____

_____

_____

_____

_____

_____

_____

TYPICAL PRIVATE PLACEMENT PROGRAMS

Required Legal Disclaimer: Admittance to these programs is by invitation only. They are not open to the public. This is not an offering of securities. The sender of this document is not United States Securities Dealer, Broker, US Investment Adviser, Financial Planning Firm, Accounting Firm, or Law Firm and does not offer legal, tax, investment, or accounting recommendations. Nothing contained herein should be construed as legal, tax, investment, or accounting advice. We do not sell investments. We do not and will not provide personalized investment advice. We only offer research in wealth-enhancement ideas and financial education and publish opinionated information about finance and trading in which we believe our subscribers may be interested.

This message is for informational purposes only and is neither a solicitation of investment nor an offer to sell and/or buy securities. The Recipient hereby acknowledges and confirms that neither the Sender, his/its associates, nor any other person acting on behalf of the Sender has made any statement or offer in any way whatsoever that can be construed as a "solicitation." Admission to Private Placement Platforms is by invitation only.

The information herein is confidential and protected by law. It is intended for only the recipient(s) named in the email to which this document is attached. It may contain information that is protected from use or disclosure under agreements of confidentiality or applicable law. This information may also be entitled to legal protection under the United States Electronic Communications Privacy Act, 18 USC Sections 25102521. The sender does not waive confidentiality or privilege. If you have received this email in error or are not the named recipient(s), you are hereby notified that any use, dissemination, distribution, or copying of this email or any attachments is strictly prohibited and may subject you to penalties. Please immediately notify the sender and delete this email and any attachments from your computer. You should not retain, copy or use this email or any attachments for any purpose, or disclose all or any part of the contents to anyone.

THIS INFORMATION IS PROTECTED FROM USE OR DISCLOSURE UNDER AGREEMENTS OF CONFIDENTIALITY OR APPLICABLE LAW. THIS INFORMATION MAY ALSO BE ENTITLED TO LEGAL PROTECTION UNDER THE UNITED STATES' ELECTRONIC COMMUNICATIONS PRIVACY ACT, 18 USC SECTIONS 2510-2521. SENDER DOES NOT WAIVE CONFIDENTIALITY OR PRIVILEGE. IF YOU HAVE RECEIVED THIS EMAIL IN ERROR, OR ARE NOT THE NAMED RECIPIENT(S), YOU ARE HEREBY NOTIFIED THAT ANY USE, DISSEMINATION, DISTRIBUTION OR COPYING OF THIS EMAIL OR ANY ATTACHMENTS IS STRICTLY PROHIBITED AND MAY SUBJECT YOU TO PENALTIES. PLEASE IMMEDIATELY NOTIFY THE

SENDER AND DELETE THIS EMAIL AND ANY
ATTACHMENTS FROM YOUR COMPUTER. YOU
SHOULD NOT RETAIN, COPY OR USE THIS EMAIL OR
ANY ATTACHMENTS FOR ANY PURPOSE, OR
DISCLOSE ALL OR ANY PART OF THE CONTENTS TO
ANY PERSON. SENDER IS NOT A UNITED STATES
SECURITIES DEALER OR BROKER OR U.S. INVESTMENT
ADVISER, NOR A MEMBER OF NASD, AND BOTH
PARTIES DECLARE THAT THIS E-MAIL IS NOT
INTENDED FOR THE BUYING, SELLING, TRADING OF
SECURITIES, OR THE OFFERING OF COUNSEL OR
ADVICE WITH RESPECT TO ANY SUCH ACTIVITIES.
THIS IS FOR YOUR INFORMATION ONLY AND IS NOT
TO BE CONSTRUED AS A SOLICITATION FOR FUNDS
OR THE SALE OF ANY SECURITIES. SENDER IS A
CONSULTANT AND MAKES NO LEGAL WARRANTIES
OR REPRESENTATIONS OF ANY KIND AS TO THE
BUYER, SELLER OR TRANSACTION. THE
TRANSACTION CONTEMPLATED HEREIN IS STRICTLY
ONE OF CONFERMENT AND IS IN NO WAY RELYING
UPON OR RELATING TO THE UNITED STATES
SECURITIES ACT OF 1933, AS AMENDED, OR RELATED
REGULATIONS, AND DOES NOT INVOLVE THE SALE
OF SECURITIES. WE MUTUALLY AGREE THAT THIS
TRANSACTION IS EXEMPT FROM THE SECURITIES
ACT, IS NOT INTENDED FOR THE GENERAL PUBLIC
AND ALL MATERIALS ARE FOR YOUR "PRIVATE USE
ONLY". FURTHER, THIS INFORMATION IS NOT PUBLIC
DISCLOSURE AND NOT A PUBLIC OFFERING; THIS
MESSAGE CONTAINS INFORMATION WHICH IS
CONFIDENTIAL AND PRIVILEGED; AND, MAY BE
PROPRIETARY AND DOES NOT CONSTITUTE, NOR IS IT
TO BE CONSTRUED AS LEGAL ADVICE, AS PER

GRAMM-LEACH-BLILEY ACT 15 USC, SUBCHAPTER I, SEC. 6801-6809 [4] DISCLOSURE OF NON-PUBLIC PERSONAL INFORMATION. ANY REVIEW, RE-TRANSMISSION, DISSEMINATION OR OTHER USE OF, OR TAKING OF ANY ACTION IN RELIANCE UPON THIS INFORMATION BY PERSONS OR ENTITIES OTHER THAN THE INTENDED RECIPIENT IS PROHIBITED. THIS MATERIAL IS FOR INFORMATIONAL PURPOSES ONLY AND IS NOT A SOLICITATION. IF YOU RECEIVED THIS DOCUMENT IN ERROR, PLEASE CONTACT THE SENDER BY REPLY EMAIL AND DELETE THE MATERIAL FROM ALL COMPUTERS.

ALL DUE DILIGENCE IS THE RESPONSIBILITY OF BUYER AND SELLER, NOT THE SENDER. ANY REVIEW, RETRANSMISSIONS, DISSEMINATION OR TAKING ANY ACTION IN RELIANCE UPON THIS INFO. BY PERSONS/ENTITIES OTHER THAN INTENDED RECIPIENT IS PROHIBITED. THIS MATERIAL AND ANY COMMUNICATIONS ARE NEVER A SOLICITATION FOR ANY PURPOSE IN ANY FORM OR CONTENT UPON RECEIPT OF THE DOCUMENTS, AND RECIPIENT HEREBY ACKNOWLEDGES THIS DISCLAIMER AND IF NOT ACCEPTED, RECIPIENT MUST RETURN ANY AND ALL DOCUMENTS IN THEIR ORIGINAL RECEIPTED CONDITION TO SENDER. THIS COMMUNICATION IS COVERED BY ELECTRONIC COMMUNICATIONS PRIVACY ACT OF 1986, CODIFIED AT 18 USC 1367, 2510-2521,2701-2710, 3121-3128. SEE http://ftc.gov/privacy/glbact.

WARNING OF RESPONSIBILITY: From this point forward, the international codes will be strictly enforced to exclude all intruders that send out false information. Those who submit a false NCND/IMFPA,

LOI, FCO, BCL, or FCO, as well as FALSE PROOF OF PRODUCT (POP), FALSE PROOF OF FUND (POF) or other Documents WILL BE CHARGE WITH A CRIME and such will be reported to the FBI, ICC and INTERPOL. THIS IS A FEDERAL OFFENSE. This went in to effect on 15th November, 2008 after a meeting was held between the Federal Reserve, European Central Bank, Interpol, Federal Bureau of Investigation, and SWITZERLAND ART. 305 TER insufficient diligence in financial transactions and right to report. If Sender deliberately manipulated or falsified documents and submitted intentionally misleading information, thereby preventing an implementation of the respective order, the damage done, put a flat rate of 19.88% (eighteen-comma-eight-and-eighty percent) of requested net funding amount or the proposed capital expenditure will be charged. Any further claims for damages, as well as the introduction of criminal sanctions are reserved, irrevocable plus of 5% (five percent) paymaster-fee, has been credited to the bank account.

ALL FALSE DOCUMENTS WILL BE REPORTED TO AUTHORITIES

Federal Bureau of Investigation
J. Edgar Hoover Building
935 Pennsylvania Avenue, NW
Washington, D.C. 20535-0001
Investigations@fbi.gov

INTERPOL IP Crime
Unit INTERPOL General Secretariat
200, quai Charles de Gaulle

69006 Lyon, France
Fax: +33 (0) 4 72 44 72 21
Website: www.INTERPOL.int

International Chamber of Commerce
38 Cours Albert 1er
75008 Paris, France
Tel. +33 1 49 53 28 28
Fax +33 1 49 53 28 59

EXAMPLE OF TYPICAL HISTORICAL PROGRAM PARAMETERS

BY INVITATION ONLY:

AAA-1 Ppps, 500m MINIMUM INCLUDING UNLIMITED HERITAGE FUNDS. WE USE OUR OWN FUNDS TO BLOCK THE TRANSACTION. THE CLIENT'S FUNDS ARE NEVER AT RISK.

WE PROVIDE A 5 YEAR CONTRACT.

WE OFFER 8 DIFFERENT PLATFORMS.

The ideal customer is any organization (pension funds, trust funds) or individual looking to enter into Private Placement Programs, or to monetize bank instruments.

Examples include MTNs, BGs, or SBLCs, then providing a PPP opportunity.

We trade all of the Heritage Funds for all of the elders in all of the banks except HSBC, Hong Kong. The Chinese Government trades all of the Heritage Funds in that bank.

500m minimum BGs / SBLCs ARE AVAILABLE FROM TOP 5 BANKS. FC/SS MTNs COMING SOON.

WE ARE OUR OWN CUTTING HOUSE FOR ALL OF THE PAPER WE PROVIDE. WE CAN ALSO MONETISE AND TRADE if you have already been issued BG/SBLC FROM A BANK.

An example of one contract we have had is for the purchase of a BG/SBLC. This has been a private opportunity only. The price has been sixty seven percent (67%) of the face value (65 + 2).

We will Issue the 799/ 760 first and after the 799/760 is received by the client's bank, the payment will be due. The issue will be from one of the top 25 banks. The client must have the funds to purchase in the bank, as it will be verified during the due-diligence process.

The funds should be in the account that will be receiving the SBLC/ and or BG(s).

The paper is issued in tranches of 500M each.

Note: The BG/ SBLC will be issued in the client's name. The client will have the opportunity when he/she performs to continue to purchase up to 2B with rolls and extensions.

The BG will be issued in the client's name and it will be discounted and priced at sixty seven percent (67%) of the face value. The proceeds may be placed, if the client wishes, for participation in the Financial Opportunity that will be presented. A 67% LTV non-recourse loan will be given to the client.

ALL DOCUMENTS CAN ONLY BE SIGNED BY THE ACCOUNT HOLDER/ SIGNATORY/ OWNER OF THE FUNDS.

The client can use his/ her funds in any way that they choose as the agreement does not have a restriction that dictates the funds being used for projects.

The client will complete the necessary contracts prior to the 799/760 being sent.

Also the client will have to send to us a physical RWA (Ready Willing and Able). In this transaction we move first. At the end of the term of one year the paper is returned to the issuer.

If the client wants to proceed, we will need a CIS/ KYC completed and banking details to hold this position.

To start the process, only send us a CIS. Then we will send our KYC to the client. If there is any hesitation of not wanting to send us an up-to-date KYC, we will reject the client's request for any of our services.

Once we receive the KYC and all other specific documents we can proceed. The process for approval takes approximately 72 hours. Within that time period the client will receive a number of documents from us that will need to be signed and returned. Those documents will be NCND, Fee Agreement etc. We cannot complete any of those without client details. Thank you for taking the time to contact us and we are looking forward to being of service to you and your clients.

DOCUMENTS CLIENT CAN EXPECT TO RECEIVE FROM US

KYC, fee agreement, JV agreement, etc. These standard documents will be sent to the client. If you have presently a CIS or a KYC then you may send that and we will have our office to complete those on our forms and send our documents to the client to be signed.

Only the signatory of the account (Account Holder) can go into contract with us.

THE CLIENT SHOULD KNOW THAT THEY CANNOT REMOVE ANY PAGES NOR CHANGE ANY WORDING IN THE KYC. ALSO SHOULD BE SIGNED IN BLUE INK AND RETURNED TO CUTTING HOUSE BY THE CLIENT DIRECTLY FROM THE CLIENT'S EMAIL WITHOUT TRAIL OR CC/BCC.

Note: If the client has a KYC already prepared, we will accept that and transfer the information onto our KYC and other documents to be endorsed by the client.

Once engaged, the paperwork will need to be endorsed, notarized, etc. and returned within 24 to 48 hours.

Once we have received all documents, a master contract will then be sent to the client for final signature, etc. and that contract should be returned. At the end if one year the BG/SBLC will be returned to the issuer unless otherwise requested to continue or renew. Thank you.

Note: Programs come and go every month. Refer to the document "Current Programs" to find out what is available this month. The link to "Current Programs" is:

www.sirpatrickbijou.com

NOTES

_____

_____

_____

_____

_____

_____

_____

_____

_____

_____

_____

_____

_____

_____

_____

_____

NOTES

NOTES

NOTES

NOTES

OTHER BOOKS BY THE AUTHOR

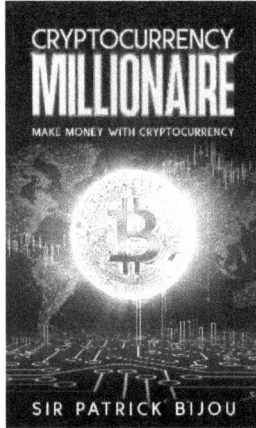

Cryptocurrency Millionaire Make Money
With Cryptocurrency

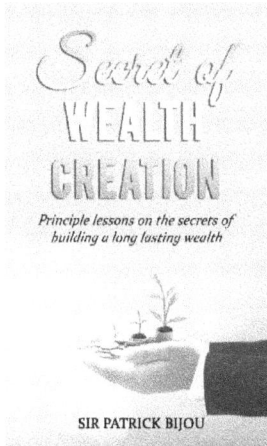

Secret Of Wealth Creation: Principle Lessons On
The Secrets Of Building A Long Lasting Wealth

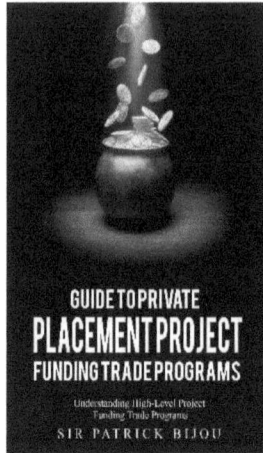

Guide To Private Placement Project Fundingtrade
Programs: Understanding High-Level Project Funding
Trade Programs

Make Money Doing Nothing

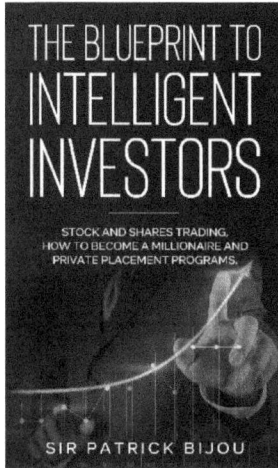

The Blueprint To Intelligent Investors

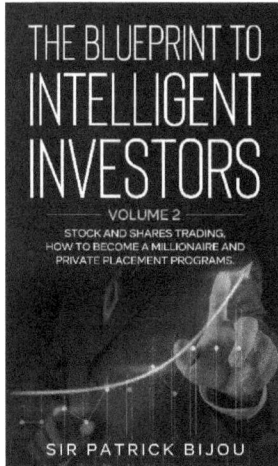

The Blueprint To Intelligent Investors Volume 2

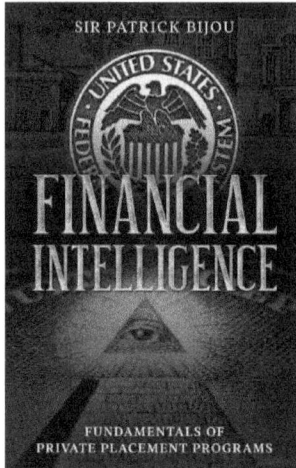

Financial Intelligence: Fundamentals Of Private Placement Programs (PPP)

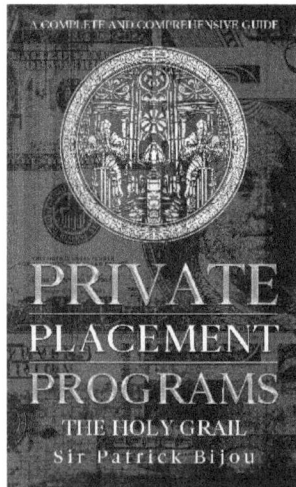

Private Placement Programs - The Holy Grail

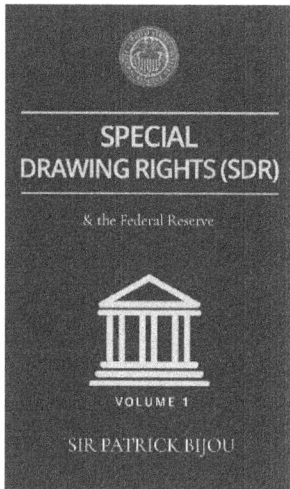

Special Drawing Rights (SDR) And The Federal Reserve

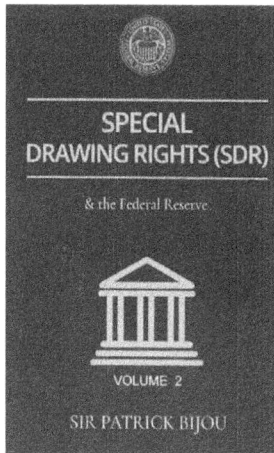

Special Drawing Rights (SDR) And The Federal Reserve Volume 2.

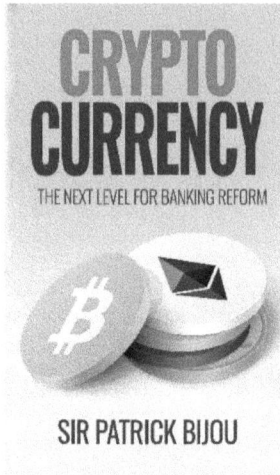

Cryptocurrency: The Next Level For Banking
Reform

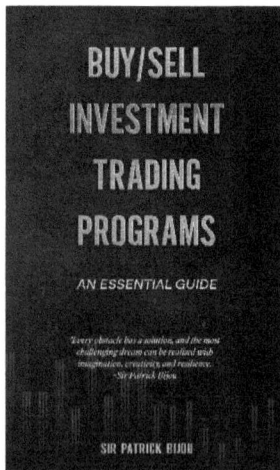

Fundamentals Of Buy/Sell Investment Trading
Programs